SLEEP BARN

Sleep Barn © Nancy Dymond, 2015

Cover Art: "Sleep Barn" by Nancy Dymond
Book Editor: Mary Olmsted Greene

First Edition, 2015
  Library of Congress Cataloging-in-Publication Data
  Dymond, Nancy, 1952
  Sleep Barn / Nancy Dymond
  ISBN 978-0-9911878-6-7   (Paperback)

Stockport **Flats** 2015

9 CHERRY HILL ROAD   NEW PALTZ, NY 12561   (607) 793-0374   www.stockportflats.org

dedicated to Randy

BLOOMING

NOISY

OH, MASTER

FOOTPATHS

BLOOMING

Weed in the garden
blooms like a flower
bright with life
I cannot pull it.

Season Ticket

ACT ONE — *Scene One*

I don't know if I will like the show
I may get up and walk out.
But I've already paid
and besides
I feel the actor's hungry eyes on me.

Scene Two

Even in the darkened theater
I feel his focused eyes.
"Who is doing the performing?"
he asks slyly.
I look at the audience
performing its itchy twitchy dance
of impatience and expectation.
It takes time to hide the manger
for the sleeping babe
to be found by the wise men.

Scene Three

St. Mary of the Moment, glittering,
twirls across the stage.
Her spinning white tutu
trails a tail of sparkles like a comet
she smiles quickly, a lightning smile,
before the darkness hides her.
(Exit stage left)
(*Spontaneous applause erupts*)

ACT TWO — *Scene One*

My grandmothers, smiling,
leave the theater arm-in-arm.
Clearly
they had never intended
to stay for the final act …

Scene Two

Onstage the hangman appears
with his noose tied lightly
around his own neck.
"Watch this!" he says
and hangs himself
(Exit through trap door)
(*No one laughs*)

Scene Three

My father limps slowly past me
along the carpeted aisle.
Seeing me, he stops,
executes a bewildered shrug.
"What's it all about?" he mouths silently
and continues toward the exit.

ACT THREE

Onstage they're playing a game.
Two syllables, sounds like, rhymes with …
I laugh and smile.
This is my game,
I whisper to everyone around me,
My game.

Reflection

Can you recognize your mother
          in her reflection?
Does she ripple with the trauma
          of your birth?
Do you see her sway in the current
          she has birthed?

Will you look up to see her real image
before her reflection fades away?

Home

I wanna go home
see Mom Dad
touch the folks
with tentacles of my life light beam
put myself like a book
before their very noses
appear like Moses

Take me in and love me
though I am a gypsy
and my life calls me away
so often
down darkest alleyways
around forbidding corners

I wanna go home
touch the folks
just to show them
I still carry their light

The Emporium of Antiques

Each narrow passageway offers its row of
curio-filled cubicles
remnants speaking softly
in the emporium of antiques

Bentwood rocker ... I remember sitting on a lap here
Now, don't get too near that hurricane lamp!
someone used to say who tucked me into
a chilly bed (birds-eye maple with matching dresser)
a hot towel-wrapped brick at my feet.

Next cubicle — the old porch swing
scene of pea shelling and string bean snapping
and there — see — even the enameled pans we used
to take the scraps across the road.

Next cubicle
filled with precious presents
erector set, bride doll, a ride-on fire truck
pink plastic figurines and chubby handled fishing poles
dominoes and tiddly winks.

Boxes
filled with penny postcards that journey
from mountain top resorts reached by cable car
to the wish-you-were-here
white sandy beaches of the Florida Keys
stopping en route to gape at the world's only sausage tree.

Books
inset with tintypes of serious stares
family group stares
men with funny hair stares
women in fancy finery stares and then

a sepia-toned portrait of a young woman
poised, mysterious, pensive
glancing to the side and up
words carefully, simply scribed:
Lest you forget ... Claire

Remembering Pumpkins

I remember pumpkins as a row of heads
that capped a fieldstone fence with blazing color,
radiant spheres with faces
glowing over growing shades of creeping night.

Companion shadows shook alive
the evening veil that quivered slightly,
shimmering 'mid creaks and snaps
of darkly curtained mischief.

In the morning we found pieces,
jagged echoes moist and shining,
saffron meat and ivory teeth —
a gleaming feast for crows.

Invasive

the guy at the nursery said
we're bringing it home on our shoes

it's the heat, the humidity
like a tropical jungle

the roots are groping tentacles
like wrapped wire

it's pretty to look at —
elongated, deep green
but it's scary

like science fiction stuff
killing everything else around

you don't want to use poison
you have to cut it at the root

it's going to be interesting
to see it die

(i think we're going to need some professional help)

Fossilized

When the world was young
it was creepy
crawly and swimmy
with slimy grooves
and blindly groping filaments

Later the swimmy
crawled on land
and became dinosaurs
the filaments photosynthesized
into large leafed plants

This would not have been
to my liking but
I wasn't there in my
bipedal omnipotence

Judging yes this, no that
naming the animals
eating the plants
tending the apple tree

I would like to think
that these fossils
have nothing to do with me
They are a study I have taken up

But when I have sat too long over my books
I start to feel crawly
my grooves begin to slime
and I realize that I am only eons
away from becoming a fossil in the rocks

Mass Extinctions

Fluted, lobed, horned ammo-
nites fighting for life
Devonian over seaing the
quick and the dead

Trilobite resting on a rock
millions of years pass
its relatives die
its few living descendants
hide in their harder shells

flourish and die
flourish and die

Exoskeletons line the
beds and quarries
prior and pooling
code lines of existence

Visit them here
in the sculptor's mind:
Corkscrew Ammonite
Crest of a Trilobite
Brachiopod Cliff

All intertwining in
that forest — the one
where a tree falls and
you don't hear it
the one you can't see
for the trees

Leaving the Empty Room

Crying.
I cannot say why.
I am just a pillar of salt
sweeping the room with my
aching searchlight.

Pages from a photo calendar
seem to fly off in the wind.
A worn and broken sofa
slides drowsily off the balcony railing,
bouncing into the dumpster below
with a clang bang finality.

Four familiar men stand and watch
reliving their buccaneer antics of childhood:
riding across the prairie on their sofa arm steeds,
ascending vertical cliffs above clouds of upholstery,
performing death defying dives into pillowed seas.

One puts his arm around me
then helps me to carry the desk
downstairs to the U-Haul trailer.
Another checks the closet.
O my god look mom —
my old orange pocket knife!

At last we are working together.
No child has been sent to stand in the corner.
No prayers are left unanswered.
This is the happy ending to childhood.

A Habit

Just a minute ago
17 wild demons stormed
into my canopy of thoughts
Ike didn't even notice
He was too busy writing
"Poems To Be Published"
looking at the teevee for inspiration
Ike is fun to live with
even if he doesn't notice
things going on around
He knows I have a habit
so he only smokes half
a cigarette at a time and
leaves the snipes for me
lying neatly beside
the ashtray
He knows I have a habit
and I'm glad he cares
because some people wouldn't
some people would make you say
please and thank you all the time
and never let you fart
or pick your nose
but not Ike
Ike knows that people are human beings
and he knows I have a habit

that boy who climbed trees

that boy who climbed trees
delighted in the quick scramble up the trunk
rough bark or smooth
the approach was the same
three steps and catapult to the lowest branch or
absent a lowest branch
as high as he could get a good clamp
for a determined shinny

his humus eyes sucked in the sky's blue taunt
as with the quick movements of a squirrel
he swung, hung, grasped, jumped his way
to the highest branch that would hold his
jaybird's weight
and sat in splendor looking out through leafy apertures
framing every cloud and bird and insect
a snapshot promenade for his kingly inspection
who can know what else that boy dreamed
as the trees planted their roots deep
in his firmament

he exhaled the soft breath of trees in summer
and sucked in the thrill of their stark
lifelessness in winter
celebrated the relentless return in the spring
of buds, blossoms, trickling sticky sap

when the leaves began to change color
it was because his birthday was approaching
no amount of science could explain that away
nor could he ever in his adult lifetime
be persuaded to believe a tree existed
for or by the simple mechanism of photosynthesis

instead uncurling within him grew
the possibility that these alluring arboreals
impeccable and impartial nurturers of life
stored the charged energy
of every moment of every day
collaged in electric space like insects in amber
a still life of vivid living
like that boy who climbed trees

Leaves Drying in the Son

like a spark, a thought lights her sputtering wit
hoarse laughter explodes, peaks and trembles,
scumbling ancient crows' feet into angels' wings

she sat there before, unmoving, unsmiling, uncaring,
but now her only son is here with her
in her back door kitchen shuttered against the harsh light,
the damp cold, the dead winter sky

suddenly
lifeless antiques dance in the fires of shared memories

husband / father long gone, sits again in his favorite chair
smoke of their cigarettes reminds them of him
and of aunt louise and uncle dave and of aunt margaret with
her jeweled cigarette holder held
delicately between her thumb and index finger,
and of boisterous aunt anne who talked like a man (and
smoked like a chimney)

laughing, coughing, hooked,
anchored in past tense their words
swirl like wisps of smoke
forming, diffusing, creating,
maintaining the memories of the senses
choking out the present
which is pain

her son is at the door now turning the knob
fine-tuning his good-bye words
hope you have a good day mom,
can i get anything for you
— just hand me my cigarettes darling before you go

leaves drying in the son

Locked In

The work of your fears
obliterates the world.

How does the kitchen, to me a place
warmed by sunlight filtered through
yellow checkered cafe curtains,
become to you a landscape of
lurking metals and pungent poisons,
our shared bed an incubator of dust mites?

The inferno of your fantasy blazes at
our favorite restaurant's candlelit tables.

Oh, how you have fought
to keep a steady step ahead of your nightmares,
word association: height, flight, water /
falling, crashing, drowning
in what future will you feel safe?

How safe am I
loving you in your world of whirling demons,
locked in your hopeful embrace?

From the Pain

Divorce me, you conceited fop, you clown!
Not marriage, but a sly deceit you played,
For far too long you wore the captain's crown,
'The Family Man,' a merry masquerade.

Believe Me, no ... no, *Trust Me* were the words
That cut the deepest once the truth was known,
Divorce me! From the saddle take the burr,
Why, take the saddle, too! Leave me alone.

You silly ass, to play me for a fool,
What do you win, I wonder, what's the prize?
What can you gain by breaking hearts and rules?
What is it that is worth a thousand lies?

In twenty years I'll find my heart again,
Perhaps create a sonnet from the pain.

What Do I Know About Cars?

What do I know about cars?
all the cars I have ever driven
have broken down
the brown Gremlin my ex drove
spun on ice
impacting a likeness of itself into the guardrail
but let's not talk about him and
all the cars and plans he derailed.

I had a yellow Valiant once —
the first car I ever bought was
impervious to being side-slammed
to being rear-ended and shoved rudely
up the concrete steps of a rowhouse
but when my ex drove it
a Jaguar ran a red light
hit it head on
totaling it
but let's not talk about him.

Piranha in the Lake

Night after night for weeks
before the wifeheart shattered,
the gentle nightsong was pierced
by shimmering moonstrings
of canine crescendo.
They who keened
outside my bedroom window
sensed the sprinting approach
of the nightmare dog — Cerberos.
'Ere he was done with us
one of that Brementown quartet
would be carried off,
eyes glazed over,
loyal tongue lolling lifelessly
beside the sacrificial corpse.

The children saw but they did not
understand the nature of a man's selfishness,
how hate swims below the surface
like piranha in the lake.

There Are No Accidents

i'm in the kitchen
when this happens

a ferret scurries across the counter
spilling the wine,
i clutch my pet

my heart — my inward heart leaps,
its sudden heat causes the water to rise
above the walls of its container

the buzzer buzzes
the lid pops off
the pot boils over

streaming rivulets invade the dark oven
where something is baking and rising
like fragrant bread

dressed in my matted and furred apron
i gape once more at the recipe
like a rabbit at a rainbow

First Wave

I'm moving out
of this cocooned atmosphere
it used to be so spacious
there were hills
crevasses and eddies to explore
but it's cramped now.

I won't be going alone
there are others
the bored and the brave
swelling with
their need to fly.

Swarms of a later generation
in a season beyond our knowing
will argue the source of this compulsion
was instinct, was fear, was courage.

All I know is
I'm in love with Mars
I bought my ticket
I'm moving out.

NOISY

Idle empty chair
Storm of silence
Too noisy
For me to think.

Remember the Abacus!

We're megabitten, number-crunched,
We're ROMMED and RAMMED to death,
We're supposed to feel the privilege of high tech,
But more often we're disgusted
By the microchips we trusted,
And we'd like to boot the whole darn thing to heck!

When Marco Polo ventured forth
For profit from the East,
Compelled by grand adventure, wanderlust,
He found that those in China
Had been counting one to nine-a,
On an instrument they called the abacus.

On a wooden frame with wires,
On which spun some colored beads,
Worked a person who was trained which way to move 'em,
Spinning hues of skies and seas,
Made the counting chore a breeze,
My question is — Why bother to improve 'em?

When man has reached his limit,
Who will have the final say?
Will robotics steal Prometheus' fire from man?
Or will humans show their might,
Pull the plug, turn out the light,
To reveal that common sense was once the plan?

Sensible Entrance

To Struggle World (clang!) World of Struggles

BIG BANG
Ears pick up (human) prick up (feral*),
Last step on the sensibility trial
(clang!) trail (bzzzz!) thread,
Aural smithy hammers out
fear / danger / warning,
Rhythm-me-call pufferations
permeate cochlear
implantation overlay.

FILIAL FLARE
As in "Walk toward the _____"
mmmmmm ... une ...
Navigate lunar loneship's general genera,
Generational orb-bits of brown, blue, green, gray, yellow (feral*),
Observational record remains intact,
Future viewers advise discretion,
Retinal profanity discouraged.

OLFACTORY PRESENCES
Taste presence / preference awareness,
Recessed mnemonic fjords
express as fragrance, flavor, nostalgia,
scenting the prey (feral*),
also prejudice.

CONTACT POINTS
Tangible relational communication,
slobber smacking petting grasping,
Stoking either the calming illusion —
tendrils access satisfaction / fulfillment pools —
or confrontational anticipation (chronic anxiety),
Experience engagement of reach / retract response,
reflexive jawsnap (feral*)

FINAL DIRECTIVE — AMPLIFY SURVIVAL PRIORITIES
(clue: define survival)

* Feral: having escaped domestication

Puzzled

Within the frame the picture lies,
Though first it's seen without the eyes,
Projected onto empty space,
An image of a scene or face
Endeavors boldly to arise.

The game's afoot, the scene's the prize,
Assembled by a mind surprised
That each small bit can find its place
Within the frame.

A thousand interlocks comprise
A pattern that not otherwise
Could be engaged to interface,
Each small success a touch of grace,
Because there is no compromise
Within the frame.

Seamless

Recognizing patterns in the random and chaotic input our five senses permit
and being able to assemble them in order to interact with them is the hallmark
of a high I.Q. For the most part, this is conducted invisibly and unconsciously, like
evolution. Similar to evolution, pattern recognition can be accelerated and enhanced by
focused and purposeful manipulation.

With pursed lips
she studies the pieces
butterfly costume emerges — but how?

Sleep Barn

Falling asleep at the sleep barn
Means death on the highway
Or at least a short detour into
A tree-lined pasture
If you're lucky.

If you're lucky and alert
And don't let your mind
Wander wondering what
Demented distractor
Placed such a sign —
Non sequitur, no context —
Where it hovers over the door
Its stark contrast to the
Gray, aging barn wood
Making it seem to vibrate
Between two real worlds

If you can defy your long-held
Habit to obey road signage
(Think: Do NOT fall asleep here!)
Then you might
Catch a quick glimpse through
The half-open door.

I've tried
How I have tried
To see and to remember
But it is like waking from a dream
Going 45 miles an hour quick glance
To the right my eyes
Have a foot inside the door
I see I gasp I reach for ...

Search in the rear view mirror for ...
Something I've suddenly forgotten
Something I should absolutely know
Something totally familiar and unequivocal.

Out of sight now there is no barn
Just a memory of a barn whose
Urgency seeps away on a blue sky day.

The Way We Sleep

Falling into bed
we feel daylight's groaning corpse
collapsing trembling rocking down the curved banister

Its silent crash splinters an entry
through thinning material of doors and locks
sweet pulses of vertigo waft upstairs

Spaces   lengthen   between   our   drawled   phrases

In a tumble of dreams blankets furl
like waves curling and breaking
over the shipwrecked timbers of our angled bodies

We   are   barely   touching   now

A cough a slight noise
churns the darkening waters
sending spars and masts tangling

From the depths a ribbed fin rises
lazily stroking the face of calming waters

Watching this moment
we two float softly down
far away from the mythical forms
of land and dry air

Dentalia's Lament

with apologies to Robert Burns (Fareweel to A' Our Scottish Fame)

Farewell to crunch and bite and chew
Farewell to tongue and palate
Farewell to textures old and new
The grilled steak and the salad
Now jagged edge and abscess wield
Sad wounds upon the fighters
And we must with our caries yield
Our place to better biters.

What fluoride rinse could not prevent
At high priced clinic visits
In niche and nook indeed commenced
To etch designs exquisite
The gums lost faith, we felt their cruel
Refusal to hold tighter
And whether they be foes or fools
They've swapped for better biters.

Would that we'd known the end to come
The friends that would betray us
We'd not have cleaved to jaw and gum
As if they were our saviors
In silver and amalgam hearts
We molars and incisors
Will ne'er forget the day we were
Replaced by better biters.

Only Words

I am words.
On casual days at home a simple sentiment,
a hey, hi, gotcha, love ya kind of warm articulation.
My mood can be benevolent and kind, but please don't cross me.
I can bite.

I like to bite, in fact, I'll gnash and bare my teeth for any
Dorothy Parker, Bertrand Russell, Gore Vidal
who stokes my font with wit. To wit, the words of Parker who said,
"Beauty's only skin deep," then by stealth rejoinder smirked
and smacked, "but ugly goes clean to the bone."

En garde! I am words! I parry thrust and drive my meaning
clear and focused to its target. But no! Don't think that I am
only cruel! For years I knew Sublime. There cradled in her arms
I died a million tearful deaths, engaged in lofty rhetoric
and to this day I keep a lock of her aesthetic in my phrase.

But I am words! I need, require much more than heart to live.
I also fart and wheeze and get disjunct with Slang
whose douche bag friends toss thought wads at my sleeping syntax.

One long precocious night preceded my distinct emergence
from the goo. I do remember all the grunting, growling,
pointing, the echoing frustration from the poet at the wall.
For he had painted in the torch-fed dark the nameless
beasts he felt and saw within. His ark in silence rocked
a thought that every beast might speak its name. Voila!

I'm strapped into your future in a rocket ship you can't unmake.
You'll take me simile-ing in your travels to the stars, to hell, to Mars.
I'll be translated, conjugated, googled and interrogated.
Meaning knows and fears my power.
I am one "L" short of being the entire world.

But you, my friend, have nothing to fear.
You know ...
I'm only words.

Losing Face

We
know all about losing face,
We who've ridden in humvees over mined roads
who've awakened blind, deaf, and dumb
with a breathing tube inserted in our windpipes
We know all about losing
Face.

A man without a face
is a man who butts up against the world
head butts the world
wears his faceless nonface
maskless non-mask all year
way past
Halloween.

Maybe this man with no face
who lost his face defending his country
could be elected President.
Maybe people would do an about face:
facing away from apathy
or maybe they would turn their faces away
from a countenance whose nose
is a wild-haired triangle
grown from ear cartilage
covered with forehead
Skin.

Tell you one thing
this world would be a better place
without faces that lie to your face and
Smile.

I don't mean to scare you but I know the future
I sat close to the TV last night
listening with my good
Ear.

Cosmetics

I stand before the mirror wand upraised
To blacken, lift, and separate each lash.
My pale and common hairlets darkly glazed
Thus play a part aside from their true task.
I pause to ask what subtle lack demands
This transformation by a tube of tar.
There's dignity in being who I am
With features different from a movie star.
For whom am I disguised, I ask myself.
My family and my friends know me by heart.
Toward what false end this calculated stealth?
Authentic truth abhors cosmetic art!
I'd banish all these efforts to pretend,
If only truth would be a better friend.

Shipping and Receiving

A green sticker means ship to Panama,
A red one exports to Brazil,
A yellow patch sends it to Uruguay,
There are thousands of orders to fill.

My husband's employed at the warehouse,
He makes twenty thousand a day,
You'd think he'd be tickled to work there,
Great hours, great boss and great pay.

The thing is the place has robotics
That pack, wrap and seal every flap,
Steel arms grab each widget that goes by
And rolls it in clear bubble wrap.

Light sensors can read every color
And each widget carries a dot
Signifying its next destination
And making it easy to spot.

My husband's a little bit nervous
To work near those half ton steel claws,
One time — never mind — let's just say
He discovered a serious flaw.

He found that the sensors saw color,
But couldn't tell widgets from men,
Siberia taught him a lesson,
He'll never wear purple again.

Lichen Maze

Ripples of dark advance — reverse
Ripples of light retreat — reply
Echoing moon they glide — respond
Making a liquid sound — restrain
Curving away from the edge — restrict
Parallels pooling avoid / react

Still in the midpoint an arc reforms
After the center the same retracts
Revising reviewing the scene intact
Visually cueing their mark re-aim
Seeking their opposite shore rename

Eye of the hurricane stares: reflect
By lunar momentum compelled: constrain
Transition to lichen maze base complete
Ripples of dark advance / *Repeat*

Spring Cleaning

Cloaked all winter in cozy darkness
Little spiders swing on their silken vines
Unmolested, the stale air in the house
Tumbles currents of tiny debris into
Tight corners and somehow I ignore it all
Even when I'm tripping over it! Until spring's
Reveille sweeps me lightly off my feet.

OH, MASTER

Oh, Master! Not me!
Please not alone!
Oh, Master
My first tiny step.

Home Body

In my / our safe cocoon riding
i / we for generations have had a free ride,
my / our umbilical membranes anchored in the nutrient-rich
soil / soul of my / our nurturing foundation / host.

In the beginning i / we,
one with the joy-filled body from which we took our life,
had no thought
but performed our slow climb through life
(a natural process)
rumbling and shaking to relieve tension
stopping and feeding to build strength.

But recently

what i / we called
the universal silence has expanded
into low and frequent moans that
wake me / us from our buzzing dreams
causing me / us to cast a growing eye / intention
toward undesired leaving.

Why in these last days should my / our swimmers' memories,
soft nostalgia of green and gracious firmament,
be impaled upon sharp urges
of escape / flight
from real dreams of sadly shadowed, crumpled earth
and dark, deflated promise?

Man Walks into a Bar

Man walks into a bar
expecting to see a midget
a dog with a banana, a gorilla or an alligator
these regulars no longer make him laugh
he's played out, jaded
tired of acting surprised

Man walks into a bar
just wants a drink this time
he orders a beer
a parrot on a swing serves him
but he doesn't speak
just stares into his drink
Awwwk! Squawks the parrot
unfazed, recovers the punchline
Bet you thought the horse would never sell!

Man walks into a bar
I get no respect he thinks
adjusting the steering wheel
he's stuffed into his pants
It's driving me nuts

Man walks into a bar
takes a table in a dark corner
keeps his back up against the wall
watches the door
in walk a priest, a rabbi, a nun, a doctor, an engineer and a blond,
The bartender says
Hey, what is this, some kind of a joke?

Man walks into a bar
Ouch.

Worthless Junk

Imagination lives in harmony with Junk.
She's Junk's best friend and greatest enabler.
Junk lies snoring on the couch. She wraps him in colored tissue paper.
Junk slouches like a pile of books in the corner. She lovingly
impales him on a lamp stand and slaps a beaded shade on his head.
Junk beckons from the sidewalk. She fetches him home.

Imagination follows Junk everywhere,
surprises him with a pastiche parfait —
layered bits of driftwood, a feather, shiny stones
inside his glass half-empty.

They lie in bed together dreaming of the Great Pacific Garbage Patch
all that flotsam and jetsam tangling slowly in the currents.
Their long-term goal is to become a famous work of art
that is never finished, that just keeps on collaging.

Imagination waves away her friends' concerns that
Junk will never change; he'll always be someone's castoff carpet,
forsaken quilt, a hose reel without a handle. Her friends will
never understand. That's exactly what she loves about him.

Suzannah Gal
(aka Fly Around My Pretty Little Miss)

The girl in the blue bandanna
leans forward to hear a secret.

The masked man's mouth is duct-taped shut
His hat is green
His nose is blue, like her bandanna
A silent cardinal is peering into her brain
What he has seen has killed him
His red feathered body protrudes stiffly
from a fold in her bandanna
and still she looks hopefully at that masked bandit
as if he might yet share with her the exit joke —
the last thing she needs to know — but no,
it's too late.

His spirit ascends the broomstick of his body
like a brown tornado
and his memories — a rising cloud of houses, horses,
dogs and women, cars, bars and gurus —
leak out behind him.

Her left eye corked, the girl leans forward
till the blue of her bandanna touches
the green hat
I love you but stay where you are she seems to say
flippantly tossing
that mane of brown hair
Her hands roll
the purple door
into place between them.

Something has been sealed off
and something has been revealed.

Something remains bound
but something is free at last.

For Lillie

A girl
is furnished by God
with the power to endure
the searing,
unpredictable
heat of experience.
Rough shapes of primal impulse
draw their longings for beauty
from the emanating rhythms
of her slow dance
upon the face of the waters ...

Sparkling, holy, wholly wedded,
nuptial gown continually threaded,
lashed but lifted by the dreaded
force which spins the life wheel faster
animates the alabaster.
Girl to woman thus ascends
to incarnate all dreams. Amen.

The Muse's Dorothy

I've seen you consulting with your muse
she seems to be always with you
on your left shoulder
I've seen your eyes shift for a second
before you speak.

Your words are
shapes that glide and peak
drawing her landscape
into the room
I can almost see her
a pause in your speech
a catch in your breath.

I wish my muse were so present
whispering in my ear
calling beautiful sounds
the way ethereal aromas
like the perking of coffee
or chocolate cake baking in the oven
colors stale air.

My First Enemy

Today the gazing globe you made for my birthday
gleams in the grass; its grout-set gems issue
bright sparkles to spin beside our sadness.
A plaque glints on the stone where our father's ashes
nourish the roots of the mulberry tree.

Our wise and brilliant mother sets a lunch of cold cuts
before us, her first and second daughters.
She laughs as we entertain each other with remembrances;
produces peacock feather wands to balance on our palms.

We high-five each other's
rapid-fire solutions to the woes of the world:
    Duh ... simple! Siphon the Mississippi River's overflow
    to quench the raging fires in Arizona! People! We're job creatin' here!
    Everyone, who's not already, start suckin' now!

Oh, my sister,
the gifts rough and sanded that you have given me
all my life (save my first 2 years as an only child)
have blessed me. But I knew from the start you would bring trouble.

I knew your kind of trouble well enough at 2 years
to spit on your imp's face when Mom brought you
home to my house from the hospital. Throughout our childhood
your effortless cartwheels made you my sworn enemy.

My enemy twirls wantonly through our mother's kitchen casting love about loosely. She recites Hafiz while spinning:

Joy
Is the royal garment

And now every day I could wear
That regal
Coat,

But I so love the common man
And feel for all
Their labor

I often paint a vast drop
Of compassion
In

My
*Eye.**

* *That Regal Coat from "The Gift: Poems by Hafiz the Great Sufi Master,"*
translated by Daniel Ladinsky

Unpredictable

She used her gypsy ball to make decisions
it was a ritual that had rules
close your eyes
      shake the ball seven times
            turn it over to read the answer
It says
  NOT READY YET
At first it was a game
her friends played too
      shake the ball seven times
          turn it over

ASK AGAIN LATER

Should I go to the prom with Teddy?
when the stars said NO
she stayed home

Should I take a summer job?
BETTER NOT TELL YOU NOW
She cautiously declined the offer

In her senior year of high school
the ball encouraged her
YOU MAY RELY ON IT (red outfit today?)
INDICATIONS SAY YES (after school parkour?)
YES— DEFINITELY (she got engaged to Brian)

Brian was slightly disappointed
when she insisted on choosing his best man
he noticed unhappily that
the groomsmens' lavender tuxedos
clashed mightily with her
Rustoleum red wedding gown

The gypsy ball told the sexes of her two children
approved their names
chose their godparents
all in secret by now
because of Brian

Because of Brian
she was forced into the closet
her every decision
assumed an air of conspiracy
felt like a radical act

She decided to ask about the future of her marriage

 When
ASK AGAIN LATER
CANNOT PREDICT NOW
REPLY HAZY TRY AGAIN
became
MOST LIKELY
PROSPECT GOOD
she began to look at
the fireplace poker in a new way

One night when the children were
sleeping at Grandma's (SIGNS POINT TO YES)
she confronted Brian (SO IT SHALL BE)
his mouth tightened when he saw it
        shake the ball seven times
                turn it over

I thought you were done with this

She reached for the poker
knelt on the hearth beside the gypsy ball
and made up her own mind
for the first time
ever

Etiquette

This morning she got up smiling to make her husband's ham sandwich like she did every day,
One slice of white american on a bed of iceberg lettuce, lots of mayo on whole wheat,
Handed him the ziplocked bag, fat with 2 halves cut on the diagonal,
One half for lunch and one for later.
Thank you for making my sandwich he said as he says every morning.
My pleasure she answered, smiling at him again.

They had not always spoken so politely to each other.

Maneuvering in a world of someone else's expectations can be daunting,
This is hindsight talking about twice divorced lovers fearing love's lesions had
Put them beyond any possibility of making 'the right choice,'
Fearing that they may have settled for less than they really wanted, really deserved,
Finding that someone else's children were like speed bumps in the neighborhood of romance,
But needing someone to care about their daily concerns, someone to hold at night,
They made the 'right choice' praying
That everything they had learned from past loves might serve them.
As the baggage was being redistributed there was a time during which

They had not always spoken so politely to each other.

Pick me up later, he reminded her. *I have an appointment with the dentist.*
A bunch of teeth had fallen out of his mouth all at once — surprise — no chewing on the left.
Nothing had happened in ten years except they had grown slower to anger and quieter,
Had settled in to knowing that making the 'right choice'
Was really more a matter of making the choice right.
I'll be there, she answered kindly and he knew that she would.
How could it ever have been that

They had not always spoken so politely to each other.

How Will I Know If I Have Alzheimer's?

How will I know if I have Alzheimer's?
Whose name will I not be able to recall?
Will I awaken suddenly and leave the house in my pajamas?

What will remain when my memory is gone?
Will forgetting be more normal than remembering?
Whose name will I not be able to recall?

Will my family conspire against me?
Can love survive such a jolt?
Will forgetting be more normal than remembering?

Will I know when it's time to surrender my car keys?
Will I believe my husband is my enemy?
Can love survive such a jolt?

Will house guests converse as if I weren't here?
Who will remind me to take my pills?
Will I believe my husband is my enemy?

Will I be locked away in a house of strangers?
Where will I search for a reason to live?
Who will remind me to take my pills?

Will my poetry be left stuttering in amazed aloneness?
How will I know if I have Alzheimer's?
Where will I search for a reason to live?
Will I awaken suddenly and leave the house in my pajamas?

Oarigame

with shiny paper
i craft
tiny life boats

keenly awake
in their frothy firmament
my little boats
rock over choppy swells
blinking
like surprised and fallen stars

their oars dip and wave
i pull
another sheet

Seagoing Vessel

I offer up for reflection
on the throne of paradox
the powers of belief, superstition, thought, assumption,
the colors of the visible spectrum
the rolling hills of emotional landscape
the consequence of willing.

This is the soup I eat and swim in.
With only two eyes that wrinkle and sweat,
the flotsam bumping by me
seem like chairs, spoons, shovels, pencils
I sift through the nutrients
with the wide smile of a plankton eating whale.

On the Chopping Block

A paring knife descends
to separate the zest from orange,
drapes glowing rind upon a ribboned heap
of rippling apple green.

Sweet journey of the knife excites the breath,
each tiny spurt recites its birth
in pollen brushing buzz-filled blooms,
then slow sun-mothered swelling
in rows of tree-filled groves and now
careening bits of pulp that plop and spray
tart bits of Granny Smith within the bowl.

A kiwi sheds its rough and hairy husk,
dun robes upon the festive rind and peel,
embraces plunging blade like Juliet,
surrenders emerald chunks among the sweet,
amid the sour.

Upon the chopping block exquisite shards,
a husk and rind and peel mosaic,
while in the bowl an eager spoon is poised,
strange sadness at the choice of which to toss.
Is all we throw away forever lost?

La Corona

Vessel in a vessel, current swept liberator
Poles tirelessly through a moment's door unlocked,
They call her Redeemer, she laughs,
Knowing and seeing mean the same to her.

Poling ceaselessly through the moment's door unlocked,
Darting through open windows of excitement, danger, mystery,
(Knowing and seeing mean the same to her),
Her interest in the world fascinates and terrifies it.

Darting through open windows of excitement, danger, mystery,
She wafts the fragrance of her intoxicating brew,
Her interest in the world fascinates and terrifies it,
She tips the pitcher slowly forward toward remembrance.

She wafts the fragrance of her intoxicating brew
Into clogged spaces, swirling eddies of forgetfulness,
Tipping the pitcher slowly forward toward remembrance,
She releases her compassion on the world.

In clogged spaces, swirling eddies of forgetfulness
Explode in radiance — La Corona!
She releases her compassion on the world
And all is known.

Love

makes plants grow
makes tears flow
spreads tenderness
builds birds' nests
is in us when we're born
can make us feel forlorn
is mixed up or it's pure
will find us — that's for sure!

Path of Waking

tiny piping bird songs kindle
the sun's ancient path of waking

dream-clear drumming dawn resolves
the tense night's silent tyranny
dimming the brightest lanterns
with morning spikes and sparkles

the full world lies still
drawing breath behind
trembling fluttering eyelids

new old day
familiar strangeness
beginning again

FOOTPATHS

The world was scenic,
grass-covered plains
long footpaths
taught me how to love.

Here in My Heart

Here is the promise we made
In spring
My withered heart, my wounded
Heart.

Here lie the wolves alert
In the brush
My blossoms white, my fragile
Heart.

Here hides despair, a ghost
In rags,
My darkened room, my voiceless
Heart.

Here do I pine alone
In side
My weeping vale, my secret
Heart.

complete breath

when *i-who-resists-change* spattered hot wet balls of bereavement
against distant walls
tiny cries of surprise and anguish leapt to life
like jumping beans surfing a hot rush of air
sliding sing-song in a curiously amplified exhalation
— Huh huh huhhhhhhhh...

continuing to exhale...
i-who-avoids-change expelled
a living tsunami of spirit, sputum, and tears
a salt-saturated wake pulsing forward
exhibiting in its egress
a potent production of disintegrating debris
dropping heavily out
                        and out
                             on the breath

i-who-refuses-change
saw its soft pillow
denial
take the shape of a despairing angel
saw it lifted and carried by hurricane-force winds
its white robe a flapping flag
its countenance a desperate grimace
beauty by ugly truth perforated
drifted beyond its will to be
then
still expiring
croaking one dying blast after another
escaping bliss hissed a wild idea into view
a belief that the prior world could be resurrected
by a refusal to inhale

and
tiny
i–who-entertains-the-possibility-of-change floated
in the void between breaths
sharing space with this new knowing
that
because of the nature of breath
emptiness is filled and fullness is emptied

Egress

Genesis: soft swells rise
churning a viscous ether
a simple suggestion of life
fingers plucking gently on lute strings.

Angles and arpeggios
climb and descend —
pulse pause
pulse pause.

Each pause
tests the tension of desire
against a curved perimeter
of ivory.

Each pulse sends an image
limbs seeking limits
phantoms
perambulating a dark room.

I am the dark room and
I am desire
warming and cooling
brightening and dimming.

A quickening tempo
evokes an echoing percussion
my tap and peck staccato
sounds a fanfare of emergence.

I stand blinking wet in dry air studying sudden patterns,
lines of crosshatching overhead,
a nest of feathered shadows beneath
a melody of tiny scratches.

The Road to Night

after van Gogh's "Road with Cypress and Star"

Through the filtering dusk the song
of the bush-crickets rises, flows gently beneath
the clop of hooves and rattle of wheels.
Within the horse-led carriage a recently childless
couple rides home from a visit with friends.

Peering ahead they recognize
the parson's familiar gait, a philosopher's gait
and beside him his old friend Willem,
their slow and plodding steps creating a space
for their churning debate on the need for God.

The devil has a longtime advocate in Willem
still bitter from the desertion of his second wife
and today the necessary killing of his favorite retriever.
My dear misguided friend, he is chiding the parson,
what loving God would loose rabies on the world?

The riders pause to greet the men.
They speak of the hope of rain for crops
and of the weather this time last year
and no one speaks of death.

Even Willem, uneasily complicit, just casts
a squinting look at the sky, silently rebuking the parson's
god for flooding the world again and again
in a chaos of wildly tossing currents of loss.

Soon a cool breeze spins a cordial
Fare-thee-well, gentlemen
from the deep shadows of the moving carriage
and cypress limbs tremble slightly
over the tops of the darkening fields.

Pennywhistle

With the sorcery of living breath —
draw from six, fixed
finger-sized portals on a small metal tube
the frequencies
of beasts and boasts of distant past.

Trill alive
legends of the past and mythic heroes
like the Giant, Fionn mac Cumhail's
great deed — creating the Isle of Man by
grabbing a clod of earth from Ulster
and throwing it far out into the Irish Sea.

Pronounce the bleeding, but still beating heart
of William Wallace, brave and noble Scot,
gently with smooth sounding notes
but drive the mischief of the Elfland Queen
upon True Thomas to a climax
in tangled lifts and trills
of frenzied faerie dancing.

On the tongue a tuh tuh spitting sound
describes the anguish held intact,
portrays the bitter first impact
"The Burning of the Piper's Hut,"
(foul curse upon the gloating victor's soul!)
released upon the Highland Clans
when English victors laid a ban
against the piper's spirit stirring drone.

Though Celtic tones were shaped from women's tears,
with leaving, loss, and love the fondest themes,
the mindful tunesmith's repertoire
contains a balm that's sweet to hear,
that charms the birds' replies from trees
and sets the heart aright.

Last Day Best Day

Alexandria Bay!
tosses pink rippling streamers
at the sunset sky
a toast to our last day of vacation
the day we passed up a trip to the St. Lawrence Seaway
or a ride to St. Vincent
to see the lighthouse
and ride on the ferry to Canada
said no thanks to the craft extravaganza at Stone Mills,
spent the day instead riding a whim through the
sun-spattered waves and wakes of the great river
roaring and slapping, laughing and clapping
weaving around the Thousand (or so) Islands,
through the channels
shouting and waving in the wind and sun
10 year-old Henry cautiously manning the boat
navigating paths around buoys and shoals —
48 year-old John sitting high on the back of the captain's seat
his tan muscled body straining forward
skin, boyish eyes glowing
last day best day

Winter Visit

I forgot what winter looked like
Perhaps I had read too many fall poems
Shivering at their tales of white death

Where autumn rattles a braid of dancing skulls
Directs green leaves to speckle, brown and drop
Invites the paling world to slumber.

For the sake of my injured friend I woke in winter
Crested crunchy snow hills in my high boots
Slid crazily on slick ice, laughing

Found the summer hiding places of hummingbirds
Walked in the hoof prints of night roaming deer
Turned frigid air to steam in my hot lungs.

I sang myself home sliding and crunching
Crouching here and there under ancient firs
To trace the tiny tracks of field mice.

My injured friend is feeling better now
I see my boots drying beside the door
An invitation to remember winter again.

Soup Allure

Combine the following and stir:
A fragrant powder of savory herbs
Tree nuts tossed and gently toasted
Vegetables oiled and slowly roasted
Broth of beef, honey of bee
Flake of parsley, salt of sea.

In a great pot over a medium flame
Provoke rolling bubbles of rising steam
Turn to the lettuces; wash, chop, mix
Color with celery and carrot strips
Raisins? Almonds? Olives and cheese?
Tomatoes? Scallions? All of these?

Reduce the flame to a quiet simmer
Set the table for evening dinner
A scalloped knife beside the bread
Jam to sweeten and butter to spread
What more could a person want from life
Than a salad, a soup, and a loaf with a knife?

Roadkill

We two

Our furred faces touching
our sweet scents mingling
in the day's flowering:
moist mosses
trampled grasses
fungi spores and steaming dung.

Our hoof-tipped slender limbs
emerge from living forest
advance through dappled green,
we sniff the air for danger.

Then some great Thing
pushing air ahead of itself
lifts you in your perfect leap
and rolls you roughly back to me
your neck angled to accommodate
your new sky gaze.

Wet

Humming wet rises swiftly
over broad boulders,
explores storm-stacked debris
with cautious foaming fingers,
stops to ripple 'round fat jumping fish.

"Call me River!" it shouts,
shooting up the sides of high canyons,
"Call me Ocean!" it cries,
as the moon, crooning ancient tidal lullabies,
gently rocks her salty babe within the void.

Hurried currents are the speech of wetness,
rising spouts, spinning sprays,
sun-lifted, earth-soaked, wind-hurled, fire-curled,
dancer of momentous storms
reaching and reshaping every metered verse of earth,
river sculptor, pond designer,
cool, calm brilliance in the presence of a breeze.

Only wet knows
how to widen banks and moisten dry seed pods
how to scatter glacial bergs upon a sea
how to cool an island out of liquid rock
how to bathe and nourish a world.

Kate's Expecting

Kate's expecting three of the ewes to give birth.
Time to replace the pasture gate
bent and dented by the snowplow.

Kate anticipates the swooping arrival of barn swallows
whose daredevil stunts ply open drifted memories.
Relishing the sound of rushing water
she counts 10 steps across the bridge.

Kate's expecting every natural thing
to conduct itself according to its vernal cadence.
Her warm gaze floats a path past
gleaming petals of mountain snowdrops,
scrapes gently at the last splinters of pond ice.

A clock ticks within the steady pulsing of Kate's expectations.
An old world prepares to utter a new sound.

Green Heron Pastorale

Camouflaged among swamp shoots
her hollow bill cuts an angle
from muddy shore to gray
and gathering sky.

Dappled iridescence crossing
her lichen green back
blurs her predator shape.

To her hopes she sings:

Ke-kuk-kuk! ke-kuk-kuk!
My hunting party
seeks your plumpness
Come forth
Darling Croakers

This waiting moment
full of juice
is heard underwater — two marsh frogs
change course.

Satisfied she sings again:

Ke-kuk-kuk! Ke-kuk-kuk!
Darling Croakers
My hunting party
full and grateful
seeks your blessing

The gaze of her yellow eyes
withdraws over quieting wings
rivulets of oblivion
fall from softening skies.

A Visit with Giya

Gardenia scented hugs
Against the stiff feel of
Your corset stays, your slip, dress, apron
Fragrant layers of grandmother
Rolled and pulsed, emerged
In unexpected chuckles
That mystified me as a child.

Your freckled friend Blanche Lewis
Used her Maytag agitator
As a butter churn
We children clamored to know
Can it make ice cream, too?

And when your only child, our father,
Hushed us by the creek to watch
Him hypnotize a sleeping fish
Surprise it in its element and lift
It in the air — such wondrous doings!

In the early morning
Fresh from sleep
You welcomed giggling night-gowned girls
To snuggle with you in the sheets
Just enough room — for every body.

When we arrived and when we left
You stood on the lawn
By your tall white house
Between the hills
Above the shadowed creek
Waving hello, waving good-bye.

Free Poetry

in my pocket i stroke smooth fibers
unfold a paper hammered decades ago
by a rowdy gang of times new romans

the sting of a searing spotlight
awakens a chorus of short black scars
who scramble like newly hatched turtles
across white paper quads
i walk ahead
drawing circles with my eyes
my voice smoothing a path to the sea

i watch my babies
outrun fox, raccoon, hawk and shark
i swallow hard when they fall
a few trundle to the safety of applause
beneath salt sifted waves

until this moment i have
fingered their gleaming shells in the moonlight
garnered ardent praise for them from
silent standing rocks and staring stars
smothered with kisses their baby whimperings
but tonight there was a sign to let go
a flyer signaled from the door of the Sandy Feet Cafe
it read: free poetry tonight

About the Author

Nancy Dymond was born in Pennsylvania near Lake Erie. Her growing up years were spent moving to various towns in Pennsylvania and New Jersey due to her father's restlessness, a foundation for her of rich complexity on which to draw for meaning and inspiration. Since 2002, she has been an active member of the Upper Delaware Writers Collective, a poetry critiquing group based in Narrowsburg, New York. Her first poetry collection was published in Stockport Flats' *High Watermark Salo[o]n* Chapbook Series (Volume 1, Number 6) along with poems by Lisa Wujnovich and photos of Naomi Teppich's sculptures. Dymond edited *Arts Talk*, the Wayne County Arts Alliance newsletter for two years. Three of her poems have been awarded prizes in local competitions.

Acknowledgments

Thank you, Lori Anderson Moseman and Mary Olmsted Greene, for your unwavering confidence that this book would go to press on time. Many more thanks to you both for the guidance and encouragement you have continually offered; Mary for the years of teaching me how to effectively hone, craft and revise my poems, and Lori for her incredible ability to stay immersed in the wonder of poetry while keeping a practical eye on the publishing, proofing and timeline aspects of producing this volume of poetry.

Thank you, Walter Clark, for being a partner in every sense of the word. Thank you for the time and effort you put into finding answers to my computer problems and for reading my poems with a critical "audience" eye.

Thank you, Dad (R. Lee Dymond 1928 – 1999), for awakening in me the love of writing poetry.

Thank you, Mom, for reading to me as a young child, for keeping a bulletin board of your children's poetry, and for much, much more.

Thank you, past and future poets, who sense within and beyond the world we think we know.

"The Road to Night" was awarded first prize in the annual Mulberry Writers and Poets Society, Scranton, PA, and was published in *River Rocks Anthology*.

"Cosmetics" appeared in *Artsletter*, the monthly Delaware Valley Arts Alliance (DVAA) newsletter, previous to its publication in *River Rocks Anthology*.

"Home Body" was published in *River Rocks Anthology* and was also read aloud on the radio and archived by Stanford University during the inaugural 100 Thousand Poets for Change Day.

"Leaving the Empty Room" was published in a chapbook of the same name by the Upper Delaware Writers Collective (UDWC).

"that boy who climbed trees" was published by Delaware River Press in *Poetree*, collected works of the UDWC that were read at Grey Towers, Milford, PA.

"Remembering Pumpkins" was published in *The River Reporter*.

The following poems were previously published in *High Watermark Salo[o]n*, Volume 1, Number 6 (Stockport Flats, 2007): *"complete breath,"* "Etiquette," "Home Body," "La Corona," "Man Walks into a Bar," "Pennywhistle," "Season Ticket," "Sensible Entrance," "that boy who climbed trees," and "Wet."

"How Will I Know if I Have Alzheimer's?" and "Free Poetry" were first read aloud at the Bowery Poetry Club, NYC.

"Leaves Drying in the Son" was included in a juried collaboration between photographers and poets exhibited at Marywood University, Scranton, PA.

"Path of Waking" was paired with an artwork in the *Be Mine* Exhibition at the Delaware Valley Arts Alliance, Narrowsburg, NY.

"Wet" was collaged with other poems on audio CD, *Call Me River*, for DIGit, an international film festival held in Narrowsburg, NY.

CONFLUENCE Series

Confluence occurs when two or more streams merge or when non-riverine bodies of water meet. This poetry series seeks such convergence by publishing writers from divergent communities — ecological and aesthetic. Stockport Flats' Confluence Series showcases poets from the Upper Delaware River Basin alongside poets from the Pacific Coast estuaries. Experimentalists from the Rio Grande can find a home alongside traditional bards from the Great Lakes. Reading crosscurrents carries writers into new habits and habitats.

Designed by Lori Anderson Moseman, this volume was created using Hoefler Text and Century Gothic, printed on 80lb paper by BookMobile. Cover image is by Nancy Dymond. This on-demand edition has an initial printing of 100 copies.

CONFLUENCE Titles

Permission by Mary Olmsted Greene, 2012
Borrowed Tales by Deborah Woodard, 2012
Visions of a Post-Apocalyptic Sunrise: Detroit Poems by Esperanza Cintrón, 2014
Desire to Stay by Deni Naffziger, 2014
Hive-Mind by Suzette Bishop, 2015
Sleep Barn by Nancy Dymond, 2015

Stockport **Flats** 2015

9 CHERRY HILL ROAD   NEW PALTZ, NY 12561   (607) 793-0374   www.stockportflats.org